EMMANUEL JOSEPH

Bridges Over Borders, First-World Tools for Third-World Transformation Practical strategies for infrastructure, education, and policy transfer

Copyright © 2025 by Emmanuel Joseph

All rights reserved. No part of this publication may be reproduced, stored or transmitted in any form or by any means, electronic, mechanical, photocopying, recording, scanning, or otherwise without written permission from the publisher. It is illegal to copy this book, post it to a website, or distribute it by any other means without permission.

First edition

This book was professionally typeset on Reedsy.
Find out more at reedsy.com

# Contents

1  Chapter 1: Laying the Foundation — 1
2  Chapter 2: The Power of Policy Transfer — 3
3  Chapter 3: Infrastructure: Building Pathways to Prosperity — 5
4  Chapter 4: Education as the Ultimate Equalizer — 7
5  Chapter 5: Technology Transfer and Innovation — 9
6  Chapter 6: Sustainable Development for the Future — 11
7  Chapter 7: Collaborative Governance — 13
8  Chapter 8: Economic Empowerment and Trade — 14
9  Chapter 9: Health Systems for All — 16
10 Chapter 10: Women and Youth as Agents of Change — 18
11 Chapter 11: Cultural Exchange and Knowledge Sharing — 20
12 Chapter 12: Bridging the Digital Divide — 22
13 Chapter 13: Localizing Global Practices — 24
14 Chapter 14: Building Resilience through Collaboration — 26
15 Chapter 15: Financing Transformation — 28
16 Chapter 16: Measuring Success and Adapting Strategies — 30
17 Chapter 17: A Vision for the Future — 32

# 1

# Chapter 1: Laying the Foundation

Transformation begins with a clear understanding of the challenges and opportunities at hand. For many Third-World countries, the gaps in infrastructure, education, and governance represent significant barriers to growth. However, these gaps are also opportunities for meaningful change. This chapter explores the vision of "Bridges Over Borders," emphasizing that transformation requires international collaboration rooted in shared goals and mutual respect.

Building bridges over borders demands adaptability. Developed nations have successfully implemented strategies that may serve as inspiration, but a direct replication often fails due to cultural and societal differences. Therefore, one of the most important aspects of change is tailoring these strategies to fit local realities. This requires active engagement between nations—where learning flows in both directions—and a commitment to long-term partnerships.

Another critical component is the ethical exchange of ideas and technologies. There are risks involved in technology transfer or policy adoption, such as dependency or loss of cultural integrity. To prevent such outcomes, countries must ensure that these exchanges are rooted in empowerment rather than exploitation. Policies adapted to local needs and innovations that reflect indigenous knowledge systems create a balance between external assistance and internal growth.

Finally, this chapter establishes the role of leadership and vision in laying the groundwork for transformation. Leaders in developing nations have the power to unite citizens around a shared goal, while leaders in developed nations can advocate for fairer global partnerships. Together, they can set the stage for the practical strategies that will be explored in subsequent chapters. Transformation is not a destination but an ongoing process, and the foundation laid here will determine the success of the journey ahead.

# 2

# Chapter 2: The Power of Policy Transfer

Policy transfer is a cornerstone of development, allowing nations to adopt frameworks that have proven effective elsewhere. In this chapter, we explore how First-World nations have crafted policies that ensure societal growth and stability, and how these can inspire Third-World transformation. Examples include healthcare systems that provide universal access and education policies that prioritize inclusivity. The key lies in understanding the principles behind these policies and tailoring them to fit the unique socio-economic contexts of developing nations.

One crucial aspect of policy transfer is the emphasis on adaptability. Developed nations often operate within stable political and economic environments, while developing nations face more dynamic challenges. Therefore, policy transfer must account for these variables. For instance, while a developed nation may implement policies with long-term investment returns, developing nations might prioritize immediate impacts to address pressing needs such as poverty or unemployment. Adapting policies ensures they remain relevant and effective.

Another focus of this chapter is building capacity for policy implementation. Beyond adopting new frameworks, developing nations need the resources, personnel, and governance structures to bring these policies to life. Capacity-building involves training public officials, enhancing transparency, and strengthening institutions. For example, international partnerships often provide training programs for civil servants, ensuring they have the skills to execute newly transferred policies effectively.

Lastly, we emphasize the ethical dimension of policy transfer. Developing nations must carefully evaluate the implications of adopting foreign policies, ensuring they align with national priorities and cultural values. Policies should not merely be imposed by external actors but embraced by local communities to achieve sustainable change. This chapter sets the stage for the practical applications explored in subsequent sections of the book.

# 3

# Chapter 3: Infrastructure: Building Pathways to Prosperity

Infrastructure serves as the backbone of a thriving economy, linking people, goods, and services in powerful ways. In this chapter, we discuss the transformative impact of infrastructure development, including roads, bridges, energy grids, and telecommunication networks. These elements are vital for connecting rural and urban areas, enabling economic growth, and improving quality of life. Well-planned infrastructure creates a ripple effect, unlocking opportunities across multiple sectors.

We delve into examples from First-World nations where infrastructure has fueled progress, such as Japan's Shinkansen system and the U.S. interstate highway network. These projects demonstrate how infrastructure investments create jobs, spur innovation, and facilitate regional integration. Developing nations can draw inspiration from these models while prioritizing sustainable development practices to minimize environmental impact.

The chapter also highlights challenges in implementing large-scale infrastructure projects in Third-World countries. Funding limitations, political instability, and logistical hurdles often impede progress. However, innovative financing models such as public-private partnerships and international aid can bridge these gaps. By fostering collaboration between governments, private investors, and international organizations, developing nations can secure the resources needed for transformative infrastructure initiatives.

Ultimately, this chapter underscores the importance of long-term planning and maintenance. Infrastructure projects require ongoing investment to ensure durability and functionality. Developing nations must adopt proactive strategies for upkeep, ensuring that their investments continue to benefit future generations. This principle of sustainability extends throughout the book.

# 4

# Chapter 4: Education as the Ultimate Equalizer

Education holds the key to breaking cycles of poverty and inequality. This chapter explores how First-World nations have leveraged education systems to achieve societal transformation, serving as a blueprint for Third-World countries. Examples include Finland's emphasis on teacher quality and Singapore's integration of technology into classrooms. These strategies have proven effective in raising literacy rates, fostering innovation, and preparing students for the global workforce.

Access to education remains a major challenge in developing nations. Many children face barriers such as financial constraints, geographic isolation, and gender inequality. This chapter discusses solutions to these challenges, including community schools, scholarships, and gender-inclusive policies. By removing obstacles to education, governments can ensure that every child has the opportunity to learn and grow.

We also delve into the role of technology in transforming education. From e-learning platforms to mobile libraries, digital tools have made education more accessible to underserved communities. Developing nations can invest in affordable technologies to create inclusive learning environments that benefit both urban and rural students. Partnerships with tech companies and NGOs can accelerate this transformation.

Finally, education reform must prioritize quality alongside access. Skilled educators, well-designed curricula, and effective evaluation systems are critical for producing meaningful outcomes. By investing in teacher training and research-driven approaches, Third-World countries can create education systems that empower individuals and drive national progress.

# 5

# Chapter 5: Technology Transfer and Innovation

Technology is a transformative force, capable of bridging developmental gaps and opening new opportunities. This chapter delves into the importance of transferring technological advancements from developed nations to those still grappling with foundational challenges. Technologies such as mobile banking, agricultural innovations, and renewable energy solutions have proven to be game-changers. The key is adopting these technologies in a way that aligns with the unique needs and resources of Third-World nations.

One inspiring example of successful technology adoption is Kenya's mobile money system, M-Pesa. It revolutionized financial inclusion by providing access to banking for millions, particularly in rural areas. Similarly, India's use of digital biometric identification for public services demonstrates how technology can improve governance efficiency. Developing nations can replicate these successes by fostering partnerships with tech leaders and investing in the necessary digital infrastructure.

Innovation doesn't stop at importing foreign technologies; nurturing local ingenuity is equally critical. Third-World countries can foster innovation by investing in research and development, building incubators for startups, and creating environments that encourage problem-solving. Success stories like Nigeria's thriving fintech sector and Brazil's agricultural breakthroughs demonstrate how local innovation can complement imported technologies.

Lastly, this chapter emphasizes the ethical dimensions of technology transfer. Safeguarding data privacy, preventing exploitation, and ensuring equitable access are vital considerations. By addressing these challenges, nations can harness the full potential of technology for inclusive growth, preparing them for the chapters to come.

# 6

# Chapter 6: Sustainable Development for the Future

Sustainability is an imperative for any nation aiming for long-term transformation. This chapter explores the delicate balance between economic growth and environmental conservation. Third-World nations, often rich in natural resources, face the dual challenge of harnessing these resources for development while safeguarding them for future generations. Lessons from sustainable practices in First-World countries offer valuable insights.

Take Germany's commitment to renewable energy as an example. Its Energiewende policy serves as a blueprint for nations seeking energy security without damaging the planet. Third-World nations can adapt such models to prioritize renewable energy, whether through solar, wind, or hydroelectric solutions. Investment in green energy not only reduces carbon footprints but also creates jobs and ensures energy independence.

This chapter also highlights the role of international partnerships in advancing sustainability. From global agreements like the Paris Climate Accord to regional collaborations on clean energy, such initiatives demonstrate the power of collective action. Developing nations can leverage these platforms for technical assistance, funding, and knowledge-sharing to achieve their sustainability goals.

Finally, the chapter discusses the cultural shift required for sustainable development. Communities need to embrace sustainability as a way of life, adopting practices like waste reduction, conservation agriculture, and renewable energy usage. By integrating sustainability into their developmental frameworks, Third-World countries can achieve holistic progress that stands the test of time.

7

# Chapter 7: Collaborative Governance

Good governance is the foundation of development, and collaboration is its cornerstone. This chapter examines how Third-World nations can adopt governance models from developed nations to enhance transparency, accountability, and efficiency. Examples include Estonia's innovative e-governance initiatives and New Zealand's emphasis on participatory decision-making.

The chapter explores the importance of building trust between governments and citizens. Transparent governance structures, such as open data platforms, empower citizens to hold their leaders accountable. By adopting digital tools for governance, countries can streamline processes and reduce corruption, fostering trust and efficiency.

Another critical aspect is fostering inclusive governance. Third-World countries can draw lessons from policies that prioritize marginalized communities, ensuring that all voices are heard. For instance, Canada's commitment to indigenous rights and Norway's gender equality policies provide frameworks that can be adapted to different cultural contexts.

Lastly, this chapter emphasizes the importance of international cooperation in governance. Platforms like the United Nations and regional bodies enable nations to share best practices, resolve conflicts, and tackle shared challenges. Collaborative governance ensures that no nation is left behind in the pursuit of progress.

# 8

# Chapter 8: Economic Empowerment and Trade

Economic growth is the engine of transformation, and trade is its fuel. This chapter explores strategies for building robust economies in Third-World countries through industrialization, entrepreneurship, and global trade integration. The success stories of nations like South Korea and Singapore, which transformed themselves into economic powerhouses within decades, offer valuable lessons.

Entrepreneurship is a key driver of economic empowerment. Initiatives like microfinance programs in Bangladesh and tech hubs in Africa demonstrate how fostering small businesses can create jobs and drive innovation. This chapter explores how governments can support entrepreneurs through funding, training, and access to markets.

Trade is another critical component of economic growth. By integrating into global trade systems, Third-World countries can attract foreign investment and access new markets for their products. However, this requires a focus on improving infrastructure, reducing trade barriers, and fostering competitive industries. Case studies like Vietnam's success in the textile industry provide actionable insights.

Finally, the chapter emphasizes the importance of equitable economic growth. Policies must ensure that the benefits of development reach all segments of society, reducing inequality and fostering social harmony. This holistic approach to economic empowerment sets the stage for the subsequent chapters.

# 9

# Chapter 9: Health Systems for All

Healthcare is a fundamental right that underpins the well-being and productivity of any society. In this chapter, we explore how universal healthcare systems in First-World nations can inspire reform in developing countries. Examples include Canada's publicly funded healthcare model and Sweden's focus on preventive care. These systems prioritize accessibility, equity, and efficiency, ensuring that no one is left behind.

For Third-World nations, the healthcare challenge is multifaceted. Many countries face a shortage of medical professionals, underfunded facilities, and inadequate infrastructure. This chapter discusses strategies to address these gaps, such as training local healthcare workers, investing in community clinics, and utilizing technology to reach underserved populations. Mobile health solutions, like telemedicine platforms, are highlighted as tools for overcoming geographic barriers.

Another critical focus is tackling public health crises. Developing nations often struggle with diseases such as malaria, HIV/AIDS, and maternal mortality. By learning from First-World practices, such as vaccination campaigns and disease surveillance systems, Third-World countries can strengthen their health responses. Partnerships with international organizations can also provide funding and technical expertise for targeted interventions.

Ultimately, this chapter emphasizes the need for sustainable healthcare systems. Governments must prioritize long-term investments in health infrastructure and policies that promote healthy lifestyles. The chapter concludes with a call to action for global collaboration, highlighting health as a shared responsibility that transcends borders.

# 10

# Chapter 10: Women and Youth as Agents of Change

Women and youth represent powerful catalysts for societal transformation. This chapter delves into strategies for empowering these groups, drawing inspiration from initiatives in both developed and developing nations. Women's economic empowerment programs, like microfinance in Bangladesh, and youth entrepreneurship initiatives, such as the Tony Elumelu Foundation in Africa, are explored as models for fostering growth and inclusion.

Education and skills training are critical for unlocking the potential of women and youth. This chapter highlights programs that provide access to quality education, vocational training, and mentorship. For example, Germany's dual vocational training system offers a blueprint for equipping young people with practical skills. Similarly, initiatives like Girls Who Code emphasize the importance of bridging gender gaps in technology and innovation.

Another focus is creating enabling environments for participation. Policies that promote gender equality, youth representation, and access to resources are essential. The chapter examines examples like Rwanda's impressive parliamentary representation of women and Finland's commitment to youth engagement in policymaking. These cases demonstrate how inclusive systems

## CHAPTER 10: WOMEN AND YOUTH AS AGENTS OF CHANGE

can drive progress.

Finally, the chapter underscores the importance of societal attitudes and cultural shifts. Empowering women and youth requires challenging stereotypes, breaking down barriers, and fostering supportive communities. By investing in these groups, nations can unlock untapped potential and build a future driven by innovation and resilience.

# 11

# Chapter 11: Cultural Exchange and Knowledge Sharing

Cultural exchange enriches societies and fosters innovation by promoting mutual understanding. This chapter explores how First-World and Third-World nations can benefit from sharing knowledge, practices, and traditions. Examples include study exchange programs, international conferences, and collaborative research initiatives that bridge cultural and intellectual divides.

Knowledge sharing extends beyond formal settings. Informal networks and grassroots collaborations can also facilitate the exchange of ideas. For instance, global platforms like TED Talks and open-source software communities create spaces where people from diverse backgrounds contribute to shared goals. Developing nations can leverage these opportunities to learn and innovate.

Another critical theme is preserving cultural identity while embracing change. Cultural exchange should not result in the erosion of traditions or values. Instead, it should inspire nations to reimagine their heritage in contemporary contexts. This chapter discusses examples of cultural preservation initiatives, such as UNESCO's World Heritage projects and local storytelling programs, that showcase the importance of diversity in development.

CHAPTER 11: CULTURAL EXCHANGE AND KNOWLEDGE SHARING

The chapter concludes with a vision of global interconnectedness. By embracing cultural exchange and knowledge sharing, nations can strengthen ties, foster creativity, and collectively address global challenges. The exchange of ideas is a powerful bridge that connects people, cultures, and aspirations.

# 12

# Chapter 12: Bridging the Digital Divide

The digital divide remains a significant barrier to development in many Third-World countries. This chapter examines strategies to enhance digital access and literacy, drawing lessons from nations that have successfully bridged this gap. Initiatives like India's Digital India program and Rwanda's smart city projects serve as case studies for leveraging technology to drive progress.

Access to affordable internet and devices is a key focus. Public-private partnerships, such as those between governments and tech companies, can help expand digital infrastructure. Programs like Google's Project Loon, which provides internet through high-altitude balloons, demonstrate innovative approaches to connectivity. This chapter emphasizes the importance of affordability to ensure equitable access.

Digital literacy is another critical component of bridging the divide. Training programs for underserved communities can empower individuals to use technology effectively. Examples include coding boot camps, digital skills workshops, and e-learning platforms. By investing in education, nations can build a digitally literate workforce ready to embrace the opportunities of the 21st century.

Lastly, this chapter highlights the transformative potential of technology in areas like healthcare, education, and governance. From telemedicine to e-governance platforms, digital tools can improve service delivery and empower citizens. Bridging the digital divide is not just about access but about creating a digital ecosystem that fosters innovation and inclusion.

# 13

# Chapter 13: Localizing Global Practices

The application of global strategies to local contexts is an art that requires sensitivity and creativity. This chapter focuses on how Third-World nations can adapt First-World practices to align with their unique cultural, social, and economic realities. The process of localization ensures that borrowed policies and practices resonate with the values and circumstances of the communities they are meant to serve, fostering ownership and sustainability.

One significant example is community-driven development programs in Southeast Asia. These initiatives allow local populations to take charge of development projects, ensuring that resources are used effectively and align with community needs. Similarly, participatory budgeting models in Latin America enable citizens to have a direct say in how public funds are allocated. Such practices demonstrate the power of localizing global strategies to create meaningful impacts.

Localization also involves leveraging indigenous knowledge and traditions. Third-World nations possess rich cultural heritages and innovative practices that can complement global strategies. For instance, traditional agricultural techniques in Africa and Asia have been integrated into modern farming methods to enhance productivity while preserving ecological balance. This blend of global and local approaches creates solutions that are both effective and culturally relevant.

Lastly, the chapter emphasizes the importance of stakeholder engagement in the localization process. Governments, civil society, and international partners must work together to ensure that global practices are adapted responsibly. Transparency, inclusivity, and continuous feedback are key to achieving successful localization. By bridging the gap between global strategies and local realities, nations can pave the way for sustainable transformation.

# 14

# Chapter 14: Building Resilience through Collaboration

In an increasingly interconnected world, no nation is immune to global challenges such as climate change, pandemics, and economic crises. This chapter explores the role of international collaboration in building resilience and addressing shared problems. Developing nations can learn from First-World experiences while contributing their own insights to collective solutions.

The Paris Agreement serves as a powerful example of global cooperation to combat climate change. By committing to shared goals and actions, countries worldwide have taken steps to reduce greenhouse gas emissions and promote renewable energy. Developing nations, often disproportionately affected by climate change, can benefit from technical assistance and funding provided through such agreements.

Another example of collaboration is the COVAX initiative, which aimed to ensure equitable access to COVID-19 vaccines during the pandemic. This effort highlighted the importance of solidarity and resource-sharing in addressing health crises. The chapter discusses how similar models can be applied to other global challenges, such as food security and disaster response.

Finally, the chapter emphasizes the need for regional collaborations. Initiatives like the African Union's Agenda 2063 and ASEAN's regional integration efforts demonstrate how neighboring countries can work together to achieve common goals. By fostering partnerships at both global and regional levels, nations can build resilience and create a more equitable world.

# 15

# Chapter 15: Financing Transformation

Access to adequate funding is a major challenge for many developing nations embarking on transformative journeys. This chapter examines innovative financing mechanisms that Third-World countries can leverage to fund infrastructure, education, and social programs. It explores options such as impact investing, international aid, and public-private partnerships.

Impact investing has gained traction as a means of channeling capital toward projects that generate social and environmental benefits alongside financial returns. Examples include investments in renewable energy projects and microfinance institutions. These initiatives demonstrate how private capital can play a role in addressing development challenges while offering sustainable returns.

International aid remains a critical source of funding for many Third-World nations. However, this chapter advocates for a shift from dependency-based aid to partnerships that empower recipient nations. By aligning aid with national priorities and building local capacity, donor and recipient countries can create mutually beneficial relationships that foster long-term development.

Lastly, the chapter highlights the importance of fiscal responsibility and accountability in managing funds. Transparent budgeting, efficient resource allocation, and anti-corruption measures are essential for ensuring that investments yield maximum impact. By adopting innovative financing strategies and responsible practices, Third-World countries can unlock the resources needed for transformation.

# 16

# Chapter 16: Measuring Success and Adapting Strategies

Transformation is an ongoing process that requires continuous evaluation and adaptation. This chapter explores methods for measuring progress and refining strategies to achieve desired outcomes. The use of data and metrics allows nations to assess their development efforts and make informed decisions.

The Sustainable Development Goals (SDGs) framework provides a comprehensive set of indicators for tracking progress across various dimensions, including poverty reduction, education, and environmental sustainability. This chapter discusses how Third-World nations can adopt and adapt the SDGs to guide their transformation journeys. Regular assessments ensure that strategies remain aligned with national priorities and changing circumstances.

Another focus of this chapter is the importance of stakeholder feedback. Engaging citizens, civil society, and international partners in the evaluation process fosters accountability and inclusivity. For example, participatory monitoring and evaluation initiatives allow communities to play an active role in assessing development projects, ensuring that they address local needs.

Finally, the chapter emphasizes the need for flexibility and innovation. As challenges and opportunities evolve, nations must be willing to adapt their strategies to remain effective. The process of learning and adjustment is a hallmark of successful transformation. By embracing evaluation and adaptation, Third-World countries can ensure that their development efforts yield meaningful and lasting results.

# 17

# Chapter 17: A Vision for the Future

This concluding chapter envisions a world where bridges over borders have transformed societies, enabling nations to achieve shared prosperity. It reflects on the themes explored throughout the book, emphasizing the importance of international collaboration, cultural exchange, and innovation in driving progress. The journey of transformation is framed as a collective endeavor that requires commitment from individuals, communities, and nations alike.

The chapter celebrates the power of human ingenuity and resilience. From technology transfer to policy adaptation, the stories of success discussed in the book demonstrate that transformative change is possible when nations come together with a shared purpose. These examples serve as inspiration for readers, encouraging them to take action and contribute to the global effort for development.

A call to action resonates throughout the chapter, urging readers to become agents of change in their own spheres of influence. Whether as policymakers, educators, entrepreneurs, or global citizens, everyone has a role to play in building a brighter future. The chapter concludes with a message of hope and unity, emphasizing that the bridges we build today will shape the world we leave for future generations.

In closing, this book serves as a roadmap for creating a more equitable and interconnected world. By learning from one another and working together,

## CHAPTER 17: A VISION FOR THE FUTURE

nations can overcome challenges and achieve their full potential. The vision for the future is one of collaboration, innovation, and shared success—a testament to the power of bridges over borders.

**Book Title:** Bridges Over Borders: First-World Tools for Third-World Transformation *Practical strategies for infrastructure, education, and policy transfer*

**Description:** This groundbreaking work unveils a transformative blueprint for bridging the gap between First-World innovations and Third-World aspirations. *Bridges Over Borders* challenges the conventional narrative, presenting a bold vision where collaboration transcends borders to empower nations in their quest for progress. Rooted in practical strategies and real-world examples, the book explores how infrastructure, education, and governance can be reimagined to drive sustainable development.

Through 17 dynamic chapters, the author delves into key themes such as policy adaptation, technology transfer, and cultural localization, offering actionable insights for governments, institutions, and communities. Whether it's building resilient economies, fostering equitable healthcare systems, or empowering women and youth as agents of change, each chapter illuminates a path to transformation. Case studies from around the globe serve as inspiration, demonstrating how nations can learn from one another while preserving their unique identities.

*Bridges Over Borders* is more than a guide—it's a call to action for leaders, educators, entrepreneurs, and global citizens alike. With its blend of visionary ideas and practical tools, the book invites readers to become architects of a future where boundaries dissolve and collaboration reigns. Together, we can build a world where every nation thrives, united by shared knowledge, values, and goals.

www.ingramcontent.com/pod-product-compliance
Lightning Source LLC
LaVergne TN
LVHW020500080526
838202LV00057B/6068